MAD LIBS®

By Roger Price and Leonard Stern

PSS!

PRICE STERN SLOAN

PRICE STERN SLOAN
Published by the Penguin Group
Penguin Group (USA) Inc., 375 Hudson Street, New York, New York 10014, USA
Penguin Group (Canada), 90 Eglinton Avenue East, Suite 700,
Toronto, Ontario, Canada M4P 2Y3
(a division of Pearson Penguin Canada Inc.)
Penguin Books Ltd, 80 Strand, London WC2R 0RL, England
Penguin Ireland, 25 St Stephen's Green, Dublin 2, Ireland (a division of Penguin Books Ltd)
Penguin Group (Australia), 250 Camberwell Road, Camberwell, Victoria 3124, Australia
(a division of Pearson Australia Group Pty Ltd)
Penguin Books India Pvt Ltd, 11 Community Centre,
Panchsheel Park, New Delhi-110 017, India
Penguin Group (NZ), Cnr Airborne and Rosedale Roads,
Albany, Auckland 1310, New Zealand (a division of Pearson New Zealand Ltd)
Penguin Books (South Africa) (Pty) Ltd, 24 Sturdee Avenue,
Rosebank, Johannesburg 2196, South Africa

Penguin Books Ltd, Registered Offices: 80 Strand, London WC2R 0RL, England

Created by Stephen Hillenburg.

Published by Price Stern Sloan,
a division of Penguin Young Readers Group,
345 Hudson Street, New York, New York 10014.

ISBN 978-0-8431-2127-8

13 15 17 19 20 18 16 14

MAD LIBS

INSTRUCTIONS

MAD LIBS® is a game for people who don't like games!
It can be played by one, two, three, four, or forty.

• RIDICULOUSLY SIMPLE DIRECTIONS

In this tablet you will find stories containing blank spaces where words are
left out. One player, the READER, selects one of these stories. The READER
does not tell anyone what the story is about. Instead, he/she asks the other
players, the WRITERS, to give him/her words. These words are used to fill in
the blank spaces in the story.

• TO PLAY

The READER asks each WRITER in turn to call out a word—an adjective or
a noun or whatever the space calls for—and uses them to fill in the blank
spaces in the story. The result is a MAD LIBS® game.

When the READER then reads the completed MAD LIBS® game to the other
players, they will discover that they have written a story that is fantastic,
screamingly funny, shocking, silly, crazy, or just plain dumb—depending
upon which words each WRITER called out.

• EXAMPLE *(Before and After)*

"_____!" he said _____
       EXCLAMATION   ADVERB

as he jumped into his convertible _____ and
                                              NOUN

drove off with his _____ wife.
                          ADJECTIVE

"*Ouch*!" he said *stupidly*
       EXCLAMATION   ADVERB

as he jumped into his convertible *cat* and
                                              NOUN

drove off with his *brave* wife.
                          ADJECTIVE

MAD LIBS®

QUICK REVIEW

In case you have forgotten what adjectives, adverbs, nouns, and verbs are, here is a quick review:

An ADJECTIVE describes something or somebody. *Lumpy, soft, ugly, messy,* and *short* are adjectives.

An ADVERB tells how something is done. It modifies a verb and usually ends in "ly." *Modestly, stupidly, greedily,* and *carefully* are adverbs.

A NOUN is the name of a person, place, or thing. *Sidewalk, umbrella, bridle, bathtub,* and *nose* are nouns.

A VERB is an action word. *Run, pitch, jump,* and *swim* are verbs. Put the verbs in past tense if the directions say PAST TENSE. *Ran, pitched, jumped,* and *swam* are verbs in the past tense.

When we ask for A PLACE, we mean any sort of place: a country or city *(Spain, Cleveland)* or a room *(bathroom, kitchen).*

An EXCLAMATION or SILLY WORD is any sort of funny sound, gasp, grunt, or outcry, like *Wow!, Ouch!, Whomp!, Ick!,* and *Gadzooks!*

When we ask for specific words, like a NUMBER, a COLOR, an ANIMAL, or a PART OF THE BODY, we mean a word that is one of those things, like *seven, blue, horse,* or *head.*

When we ask for a PLURAL, it means more than one. For example, *cat* pluralized is *cats.*

MAD LIBS® is fun to play with friends, but you can also play it by yourself! To begin with, DO NOT look at the story on the page below. Fill in the blanks on this page with the words called for. Then, using the words you have selected, fill in the blank spaces in the story.

Now you've created your own hilarious MAD LIBS® game!

HOW TO DRIVE A SANDWICH

NOUN _____

ADJECTIVE _____

NOUN _____

PLURAL NOUN_____

VERB ENDING IN "ING" _____

ADVERB _____

PLURAL NOUN_____

PART OF THE BODY _____

ADJECTIVE _____

PLURAL NOUN_____

NOUN _____

NOUN _____

MAD LIBS
HOW TO DRIVE A SANDWICH

Even though SpongeBob doesn't need a/an _____'s license
NOUN

to drive around in the Patty Wagon, he still tries to observe these

_____ rules of the road:
ADJECTIVE

1. Don't drive your sandwich faster than the _____ ahead
NOUN

of you.

2. Keep a few spare _____ in the trunk in case one of
PLURAL NOUN

your pickles goes flat.

3. Remember to change the overhead grease traps often to keep the

Patty Wagon _____ _____.
VERB ENDING IN "ING"   ADVERB

4. If you ever get lost, don't be embarrassed to ask for

_____. Most folks will be happy to lend a/an
PLURAL NOUN

_____ and point you in the _____ direction.
PART OF THE BODY   ADJECTIVE

5. Be sure to signal to other _____ on the street before
PLURAL NOUN

making a left or right _____.
NOUN

6. Most importantly, always fasten your safety _____!
NOUN

MAD LIBS® is fun to play with friends, but you can also play it by yourself! To begin with, DO NOT look at the story on the page below. Fill in the blanks on this page with the words called for. Then, using the words you have selected, fill in the blank spaces in the story.

Now you've created your own hilarious MAD LIBS® game!

"WHY I LOVE WORK"
BY SPONGEBOB SQUAREPANTS

ADJECTIVE _____

NOUN _____

NOUN _____

NOUN _____

NUMBER_____

PLURAL NOUN_____

ADJECTIVE _____

NUMBER_____

NOUN _____

ADJECTIVE _____

ADJECTIVE _____

ADJECTIVE _____

PLURAL NOUN_____

PLURAL NOUN_____

NOUN _____

MAD LIBS®
"WHY I LOVE WORK"
BY SPONGEBOB SQUAREPANTS

Of all the things in this _____ world, you know what I
ADJECTIVE

love most? Working! I wake up every day before the _____
NOUN

rises and run to the Krusty Krab. I practically knock down the

_____ to get in! The first person I see is my good ol'
NOUN

_____ Squidward at the cash register, and I slap him a high
NOUN

_____. Then I salute Mr. Krabs, who taught me everything
NUMBER

I know about _____. Mr. Krabs is a/an _____
PLURAL NOUN   ADJECTIVE

boss. One time he decided to keep the Krusty Krab open _____
NUMBER

hours a day, and I got to work 'round the _____ every day
NOUN

for a month! See how he takes _____ care of me? Next
ADJECTIVE

comes the most _____ part of the day—the part where
ADJECTIVE

I get to make Krabby Patties! I take special care to make them as

_____ as possible. I love flipping the _____ on
ADJECTIVE   PLURAL NOUN

the grill and serving up sides of _____. I can't imagine my
PLURAL NOUN

life without my job at the Krusty Krab—it would be like having an

ice-cream sundae without the _____ on top!
NOUN

MAD LIBS® is fun to play with friends, but you can also play it by yourself! To begin with, DO NOT look at the story on the page below. Fill in the blanks on this page with the words called for. Then, using the words you have selected, fill in the blank spaces in the story.

Now you've created your own hilarious MAD LIBS® game!

PATRICK STAR'S DAY

ADJECTIVE _____

PLURAL NOUN _____

ADJECTIVE _____

NOUN _____

NOUN _____

VERB ENDING IN "ING" _____

NOUN _____

NOUN _____

EXCLAMATION _____

VERB _____

ADJECTIVE _____

VERB _____

NOUN _____

MAD LIBS®
PATRICK STAR'S DAY

Oh boy. Today is such a/an _____ day. First I've got to
                           ADJECTIVE

pick up some . . . uh . . . _____ for SpongeBob at the
                               PLURAL NOUN

_____ _____ shop. I just don't remember
ADJECTIVE   NOUN

how many. I'm also supposed to do . . . um . . . something over at the

Krusty _____, but I can't think what. Then SpongeBob
        NOUN

and I are going to go _____ on fish hooks at . . .
               VERB ENDING IN "ING"

somewhere. Ooh, ooh, and then I have to eat some _____-
                                 NOUN

flavored ice cream with a/an _____ on top at Goofy
                        NOUN

Goober's. _____! My day is so busy! When am I ever going
      EXCLAMATION

to have time to _____? All this thinking has made me feel
             VERB

_____. Maybe I'll just _____ here instead and
ADJECTIVE   VERB

watch the _____ grow. That sounds like the perfect day!
      NOUN

MAD LIBS® is fun to play with friends, but you can also play it by yourself! To begin with, DO NOT look at the story on the page below. Fill in the blanks on this page with the words called for. Then, using the words you have selected, fill in the blank spaces in the story.

Now you've created your own hilarious MAD LIBS® game!

EVERYONE'S FAVORITE FOODS

PLURAL NOUN _____

PLURAL NOUN _____

TYPE OF LIQUID _____

NOUN _____

PLURAL NOUN _____

NOUN _____

PLURAL NOUN _____

PLURAL NOUN _____

PLURAL NOUN _____

NOUN _____

ADJECTIVE _____

PLURAL NOUN _____

ADJECTIVE _____

PLURAL NOUN _____

MAD LIBS®
EVERYONE'S FAVORITE FOODS

We all know that SpongeBob loves his Krabby Patties, but what are

the rest of the gang's favorite _____? Squidward likes to
                                   PLURAL NOUN

eat gourmet _____. Give him a glass of _____ to
            PLURAL NOUN   TYPE OF LIQUID

wash it all down, and he'll be as happy as a/an _____. Patrick
                                                NOUN

enjoys ice-cream _____ from Goofy Goober's, but he'll also
                 PLURAL NOUN

eat just about anything you put on his _____. Mr. Krabs loves
                                       NOUN

to eat expensive _____, but he doesn't like to spend a lot of
                 PLURAL NOUN

_____ on them, so he just makes do with leftover
PLURAL NOUN

_____. Sandy Cheeks, being an adventurer and a/an
PLURAL NOUN

_____, needs to eat _____ foods, such as
NOUN   ADJECTIVE

seeds, nuts, and _____. And most Bikini Bottomites prefer
                 PLURAL NOUN

_____ Patties with _____ on top over all other
ADJECTIVE   PLURAL NOUN

foods—just like SpongeBob!

MAD LIBS® is fun to play with friends, but you can also play it by yourself! To begin with, DO NOT look at the story on the page below. Fill in the blanks on this page with the words called for. Then, using the words you have selected, fill in the blank spaces in the story.

Now you've created your own hilarious MAD LIBS® game!

THINGS THAT ANNOY SQUIDWARD

NOUN _____

VERB ENDING IN "ING" _____

NOUN _____

VERB _____

NOUN _____

ADJECTIVE _____

PLURAL NOUN _____

VERB _____

PLURAL NOUN _____

VERB _____

VERB _____

VERB _____

ADJECTIVE _____

Squidward Tentacles is annoyed by just about every single

_____ around him. Here is a list of the things that annoy
____NOUN

him the most:

1. Going _____ with SpongeBob and Patrick at Jellyfish
__VERB ENDING IN "ING"

   Fields. Understandable, as once a jellyfish stung him right on his

   _____!
   __NOUN

2. The way SpongeBob always seems to drop in for a visit while he is

   trying to _____ in the _____. Nothing
   _____VERB _____NOUN

   like hearing that high-pitched voice shout, "Hi, _____
   _____ADJECTIVE

   neighbor!" when you're washing behind your _____!
   _____PLURAL NOUN

3. The way SpongeBob likes to _____. It sounds like
   _____VERB

   _____ scratching a chalkboard. It makes
   ____PLURAL NOUN

   Squidward's skin _____. The way SpongeBob
   _____VERB

   likes to _____ bothers him, too. Or _____.
   _____VERB _____VERB

   Actually, I guess you could say the number one thing that makes

   Squidward go _____ is . . . SpongeBob SquarePants!
   ____ADJECTIVE

MAD LIBS® is fun to play with friends, but you can also play it by yourself! To begin with, DO NOT look at the story on the page below. Fill in the blanks on this page with the words called for. Then, using the words you have selected, fill in the blank spaces in the story.

Now you've created your own hilarious MAD LIBS® game!

PLANKTON'S MASTER PLAN

ADJECTIVE _____

ADJECTIVE _____

NOUN _____

PLURAL NOUN _____

PLURAL NOUN _____

PLURAL NOUN _____

VERB ENDING IN "ING" _____

PLURAL NOUN _____

PLURAL NOUN _____

OCCUPATION _____

NOUN _____

NOUN _____

NOUN _____

MAD LIBS
PLANKTON'S MASTER PLAN

I've finally done it! I've come up with a/an _____ master
ADJECTIVE

plan for taking over the world! First, I must steal the secret formula

for Mr. Krabs's _____ Patties. This will be very easy to do if
ADJECTIVE

I can acquire Neptune's royal _____, because then I'll have
NOUN

all the _____ of the sea at my beck and call! Once I have
PLURAL NOUN

the recipe, I'll need a million metal _____ for my customers
PLURAL NOUN

to wear on their _____. They won't know that there will be
PLURAL NOUN

small _____ devices inside that will allow me to
VERB ENDING IN "ING"

control their _____! Once I have these _____
PLURAL NOUN   PLURAL NOUN

at my command, everyone will treat me like a/an _____
OCCUPATION

and call me "Your Royal _____!" And the best part—I'll
NOUN

finally be the Supreme _____ of the _____!
NOUN   NOUN

From SPONGEBOB SQUAREPANTS™ MAD LIBS® • © 2006 Viacom International Inc.
All Rights Reserved. Nickelodeon, SpongeBob SquarePants and all related titles, logos and characters
are trademarks of Viacom International Inc. Published by Price Stern Sloan, a division of
Penguin Young Readers Group, 345 Hudson Street, New York, New York 10014.

MAD LIBS® is fun to play with friends, but you can also play it by yourself! To begin with, DO NOT look at the story on the page below. Fill in the blanks on this page with the words called for. Then, using the words you have selected, fill in the blank spaces in the story.

Now you've created your own hilarious MAD LIBS® game!

"ODE TO MONEY"
BY EUGENE KRABS

ADJECTIVE _____

ADJECTIVE _____

PLURAL NOUN _____

ADJECTIVE _____

NOUN _____

PLURAL NOUN _____

SILLY WORD _____

PLURAL NOUN _____

EXCLAMATION _____

ADJECTIVE _____

ADJECTIVE _____

MAD LIBS

"ODE TO MONEY"

BY EUGENE KRABS

Oh my money, my _____, _____ dollar bills!
ADJECTIVE   ADJECTIVE

How I love the way you look—green like the growing _____
PLURAL NOUN

on the seafloor.

How I love the way you feel—_____ and papery, like a/an
ADJECTIVE

_____.
NOUN

How I love the way you smell, like fresh _____ in the
PLURAL NOUN

morning.

How I love the way you sound. As I count each dollar bill, I hear

"Swish, swish, _____," like _____ swimming by.
SILLY WORD   PLURAL NOUN

How I love the way you taste, like . . . _____! Well,
EXCLAMATION

I guess you don't taste very good. But I still love you, anyway. My

_____, _____ money!
ADJECTIVE   ADJECTIVE

MAD LIBS® is fun to play with friends, but you can also play it by yourself! To begin with, DO NOT look at the story on the page below. Fill in the blanks on this page with the words called for. Then, using the words you have selected, fill in the blank spaces in the story.

Now you've created your own hilarious MAD LIBS® game!

TALK LIKE MR. KRABS

ADJECTIVE _____

NOUN _____

SAME NOUN _____

EXCLAMATION _____

PLURAL NOUN _____

VERB ENDING IN "ING" _____

PLURAL NOUN _____

PLURAL NOUN _____

ADJECTIVE _____

NOUN _____

YOUR NAME _____

MAD LIBS®

TALK LIKE MR. KRABS

Mr. Krabs has a nautical way with words! If you want to talk like Mr.

Krabs or one of his old navy buddies, just follow the _____
_____ATELINE_____

rules below!

1. Call everyone "matey" or "_____." Instead of saying
   _____NOUN_____

   "Good morning, friend," say, "Ahoy there, _____!"
   _____SAME NOUN_____

2. When you are surprised, don't say, "_____!" Instead,
   _____EXCLAMATION_____

   say, "Shiver me _____!" or "_____
   _____PLURAL NOUN_____   _____VERB ENDING IN "ING"_____

   _____!"
   _____PLURAL NOUN_____

3. When you make a promise, make a sailor's promise. Say, "Yo ho, yo

   ho, near the _____ I'll never go!"
   _____PLURAL NOUN_____

4. Get yourself a/an _____ nickname. Mr. Krabs's nickname
   _____ADJECTIVE_____

   is "Armor Abs" Krabs. Once you learn to talk like him, your name

   can be "_____-face" _____!
   _____NOUN_____   _____YOUR NAME_____

MAD LIBS® is fun to play with friends, but you can also play it by yourself! To begin with, DO NOT look at the story on the page below. Fill in the blanks on this page with the words called for. Then, using the words you have selected, fill in the blank spaces in the story.

Now you've created your own hilarious MAD LIBS® game!

GARY, COME HOME

ADJECTIVE _____

NOUN _____

PLURAL NOUN _____

NOUN _____

ADVERB _____

VERB (PAST TENSE) _____

NOUN _____

ADJECTIVE _____

PLURAL NOUN _____

NOUN _____

NOUN _____

PLURAL NOUN _____

NOUN _____

VERB _____

NOUN _____

NOUN _____

PLURAL NOUN _____

MAD LIBS®
GARY, COME HOME

Oh no! I just came home from a/an _____ day at the
                                        ADJECTIVE

Krusty _____, and Gary is nowhere to be found. Could he
            NOUN

have run away again? I know I forgot to put _____ in his
                                                  PLURAL NOUN

bowl because I was out trying to win the _____ Boy
                                                  NOUN

Challenge yesterday, but I apologized _____. I didn't mean
                                          ADVERB

to let Gary nearly starve while I _____ all day. I just forgot.
                                    VERB (PAST TENSE)

I should never have let him out of my _____. Oh, Gary,
                                            NOUN

I'm so _____! Where, oh where, could he be? What if he
          ADJECTIVE

was kidnapped by a gang of _____? Or what if he's lost in
                                PLURAL NOUN

a/an _____ shop in Shell City? What if he's gone forever?
          NOUN

I'll never hear the sweet sound of his _____ again
                                            NOUN

or watch as he ties his _____. I'll never be able to love
                          PLURAL NOUN

another _____ for as long as I _____. Wait.
            NOUN   VERB

What's that? I just heard someone knocking on the _____.
                                                        NOUN

Gary? Is it really you? Just nod your _____ if you're going
                                          NOUN

to stay. Oh, hoppin' _____! Welcome home, Gary!
                        PLURAL NOUN

MAD LIBS® is fun to play with friends, but you can also play it by yourself! To begin with, DO NOT look at the story on the page below. Fill in the blanks on this page with the words called for. Then, using the words you have selected, fill in the blank spaces in the story.

Now you've created your own hilarious MAD LIBS® game!

"HOW TO BE A GOOD NEIGHBOR"
BY SPONGEBOB SQUAREPANTS

PLURAL NOUN _____

ADJECTIVE _____

ADJECTIVE _____

ADJECTIVE _____

NOUN _____

NOUN _____

NOUN _____

NOUN _____

NUMBER _____

NUMBER _____

ADVERB _____

NOUN _____

NOUN _____

NOUN _____

NUMBER _____

ADJECTIVE _____

NOUN _____

ADJECTIVE _____

NOUN _____

MAD LIBS
"HOW TO BE A GOOD NEIGHBOR"
BY SPONGEBOB SQUAREPANTS

Greetings, boys and _____! Today I want to share some
_____ PLURAL NOUN

_____ tips on how to be a/an _____ neighbor! As
ADJECTIVE ADJECTIVE

Squidward can tell you, I am a very _____ and considerate
ADJECTIVE

_____. So, here goes!
NOUN

1. If your neighbor's morning news-_____ is accidentally
NOUN

delivered to your front _____, immediately knock
NOUN

on his or her front _____ at least _____ times.
NOUN NUMBER

If nobody answers, ring the doorbell _____ times. If no
NUMBER

one answers again, _____ yell, "I'm just gonna leave your
ADVERB

paper on the _____ step, okay?"
NOUN

2. On Sundays, refrain from playing a/an _____ outside your
NOUN

neighbor's _____ until at least _____ o'clock.
NOUN NUMBER

3. When a/an _____ neighbor moves into town, bake a
ADJECTIVE

delicious _____ and bring it over. Knock on the front
NOUN

door and say, "Welcome to our _____ _____!"
ADJECTIVE NOUN

MAD LIBS® is fun to play with friends, but you can also play it by yourself! To begin with, DO NOT look at the story on the page below. Fill in the blanks on this page with the words called for. Then, using the words you have selected, fill in the blank spaces in the story.

Now you've created your own hilarious MAD LIBS® game!

"SUNDAYS"
BY SPONGEBOB SQUAREPANTS

EXCLAMATION _____

ADJECTIVE _____

ADVERB _____

ADJECTIVE _____

NOUN _____

NOUN _____

EXCLAMATION _____

ADJECTIVE _____

ADVERB _____

NOUN _____

ADJECTIVE _____

ADJECTIVE _____

ADJECTIVE _____

PLURAL NOUN _____

MAD LIBS®
"SUNDAYS"
BY SPONGEBOB SQUAREPANTS

Oh boy, do I love Sundays! I love to wake up early—7 a.m. to be

exact—and say, "_____!" to my _____ neighbor
                       EXCLAMATION   ADJECTIVE

Squidward! He may look like he's sleeping _____,
                                                    ADVERB

but I know that he's really _____ and ready to go.
                                   ADJECTIVE

Usually I wake him up by blowing into a giant _____
                                                        NOUN

right next to his ear. This makes him jump out of his _____
                                                              NOUN

and scream, "_____! SpongeBob, you _____
                  EXCLAMATION   ADJECTIVE

little pest!" Even though he looks at me _____, I know
                                                 ADVERB

he's really thinking, *Thank you, you adorable little* _____.
                                                               NOUN

That's why I make sure to wake him up bright and _____
                                                         ADJECTIVE

every Sunday. Today, as a/an _____ surprise, I'll take him
                                   ADJECTIVE

to the Krusty Krab for _____ Patties and _____.
                              ADJECTIVE   PLURAL NOUN

I'm sure he'll love seeing Mr. Krabs on his day off. So, cancel all your

Sunday plans, Squidward, because SpongeBob's comin' over—woo-

hoo!

MAD LIBS® is fun to play with friends, but you can also play it by yourself! To begin with, DO NOT look at the story on the page below. Fill in the blanks on this page with the words called for. Then, using the words you have selected, fill in the blank spaces in the story.

Now you've created your own hilarious MAD LIBS® game!

NO MORE KRUSTY KRAB?

PLURAL NOUN _____

NOUN _____

NOUN _____

PLURAL NOUN _____

PLURAL NOUN _____

NOUN _____

ADJECTIVE _____

OCCUPATION _____

PLURAL NOUN _____

PLURAL NOUN _____

EXCLAMATION _____

PLURAL NOUN _____

ADJECTIVE _____

NO MORE KRUSTY KRAB?

Have you ever wondered where the Krusty Krab gang would work

if the restaurant went out of business? Mr. Krabs would buy all of

Bikini Bottom's _____ and charge an arm and a/an
                    PLURAL NOUN

_____ every time someone wanted to eat one. Squid-
        NOUN

ward would get a job as a musician in a/an _____ band,
                                                NOUN

and SpongeBob would do what he does best—grill _____
                                                  PLURAL NOUN

and fry _____ at another fast food _____.
        PLURAL NOUN   NOUN

Picture this: SpongeBob's cooking is so _____ that he
                                            ADJECTIVE

gets promoted to Head _____ and becomes famous for
                        OCCUPATION

making the tastiest, fastest, spongiest _____ around.
                                          PLURAL NOUN

Whenever SpongeBob's delectable _____ are for
                                    PLURAL NOUN

dinner, everyone screams,"_____! Our favorite!" Then,
                            EXCLAMATION

one day, SpongeBob's wildest _____ come true—he
                                PLURAL NOUN

goes on to become President of All Things _____ Food!
                                            ADJECTIVE

MAD LIBS® is fun to play with friends, but you can also play it by yourself! To begin with, DO NOT look at the story on the page below. Fill in the blanks on this page with the words called for. Then, using the words you have selected, fill in the blank spaces in the story.

Now you've created your own hilarious MAD LIBS® game!

MR. KRABS'S RULES

ADJECTIVE _____

VERB _____

VERB _____

NOUN _____

PLURAL NOUN _____

ADJECTIVE _____

NOUN _____

NOUN _____

PLURAL NOUN _____

ADJECTIVE _____

ADJECTIVE _____

NOUN _____

MAD LIBS

MR. KRABS'S RULES

Working for Mr. Krabs is pretty easy if you just follow his

_____ rules:
  ADJECTIVE

1. _____ on your own time—not company time.
        VERB

2. _____ more, earn less.
        VERB

3. Every time you mistreat a/an _____, that's me money
                                      NOUN

   walkin' out the door.

4. Time is money, and if you _____ are wasting time, you're
                              PLURAL NOUN

   wasting money . . . and that's just _____!
                                          ADJECTIVE

5. The _____ is always right!
          NOUN

6. Don't ever eat a/an _____ without paying for it first.
                           NOUN

   There be no free _____ at the Krusty Krab!
                       PLURAL NOUN

7. Always remember to watch out for Plankton and his

   _____ schemes. You must guard the _____
     ADJECTIVE   ADJECTIVE

   recipe for Krabby Patties with your _____!
                                          NOUN

MAD LIBS® is fun to play with friends, but you can also play it by yourself! To begin with, DO NOT look at the story on the page below. Fill in the blanks on this page with the words called for. Then, using the words you have selected, fill in the blank spaces in the story.

Now you've created your own hilarious MAD LIBS® game!

WHAT MAKES SPONGEBOB LAUGH?

ADVERB _____

ANIMAL _____

PLURAL NOUN _____

NOUN _____

ADVERB _____

VERB ENDING IN "ING" _____

ADJECTIVE _____

NOUN _____

NOUN _____

ADJECTIVE _____

ADJECTIVE _____

NOUN _____

VERB ENDING IN "ING" _____

SAME NOUN _____

MAD LIBS
WHAT MAKES
SPONGEBOB LAUGH?

When SpongeBob SquarePants laughs, he laughs _____.
ADVERB

He'll laugh at anything, too—a rubber _____, clowns
ANIMAL

juggling _____, even the old slip-on-a/an-_____-
PLURAL NOUN   NOUN

peel routine. When Patrick and SpongeBob go to Goofy Goober's,

they laugh _____ at the _____ peanut on
ADVERB   VERB ENDING IN "ING"

stage. When Sandy Cheeks attempts a/an _____ feat and
ADJECTIVE

succeeds, SpongeBob laughs with her. When she falls flat on her

_____, SpongeBob tries to cover his _____
NOUN   NOUN

with a cough. One friend who really tickles SpongeBob's

_____ bone is Squidward, who is always spouting off
ADJECTIVE

_____ sayings such as "Another day, another
ADJECTIVE

_____," which just send SpongeBob _____
NOUN   VERB ENDING IN "ING"

right into the following Tuesday! "Another day, another

_____!" Hahahahaha!
SAME NOUN

MAD LIBS® is fun to play with friends, but you can also play it by yourself! To begin with, DO NOT look at the story on the page below. Fill in the blanks on this page with the words called for. Then, using the words you have selected, fill in the blank spaces in the story.

Now you've created your own hilarious MAD LIBS® game!

FAN CLUB PLEDGE

ADJECTIVE _____

ADJECTIVE _____

ADVERB _____

PLURAL NOUN _____

PLURAL NOUN _____

NOUN _____

NOUN _____

ADVERB _____

NOUN _____

VERB _____

NOUN _____

ADJECTIVE _____

ADJECTIVE _____

NOUN _____

PLURAL NOUN _____

ADJECTIVE _____

MAD LIBS®
FAN CLUB PLEDGE

If you want to become a/an _____ member of the Sponge-
ADJECTIVE

Bob SquarePants Fan Club, you must say the following _____
ADJECTIVE

pledge:

I do _____ swear to uphold the _____ and
ADVERB   PLURAL NOUN

_____ of SpongeBob SquarePants, even at the cost of my
PLURAL NOUN

own _____. I will assist and defend the sacred _____
NOUN   NOUN

and strive to act _____ at all times. I also pledge to tell
ADVERB

all my friends about SpongeBob's great _____ and to
NOUN

_____ loudly in the living room if I ever miss a show.
VERB

I understand that SpongeBob is counting on me to carry the

_____ of comedy and tune in for _____ laughs
NOUN   ADJECTIVE

every day. I seal my oath by singing the _____ anthem
ADJECTIVE

of the SpongeBob SquarePants _____ Club: "SpongeBob
NOUN

SquarePants, hello! We pledge our _____ to the fellow, as
PLURAL NOUN

faithful as _____, as true as yellow!"
ADJECTIVE

MAD LIBS® is fun to play with friends, but you can also play it by yourself! To begin with, DO NOT look at the story on the page below. Fill in the blanks on this page with the words called for. Then, using the words you have selected, fill in the blank spaces in the story.

Now you've created your own hilarious MAD LIBS® game!

SANDY'S STUNTS

PLURAL NOUN _____

PLURAL NOUN _____

NOUN _____

VERB ENDING IN "ING" _____

NOUN _____

PLURAL NOUN _____

NOUN _____

NOUN _____

VERB _____

NOUN _____

NOUN _____

ADJECTIVE _____

PLURAL NOUN _____

PART OF THE BODY _____

PART OF THE BODY_____

ADJECTIVE _____

MAD LIBS
SANDY'S STUNTS

Ladies and _____, boys and _____, come
PLURAL NOUN   PLURAL NOUN

see Bikini Bottom's very own Sandy Cheeks attempt her most

_____-defying stunt yet. She will begin by _____
NOUN   VERB ENDING IN "ING"

on a tight-_____ over a pit of volcanic _____.
NOUN   PLURAL NOUN

Then she will climb to the top of a/an _____, dive off, and
NOUN

land on an air-filled _____. Amazingly, she will bounce
NOUN

right off and land on the floor, where she will then _____
VERB

twenty times in a circle and sing "Mary Had a Little _____,"
NOUN

all while being chased by a hungry _____ . . . and that's
NOUN

just the opening act! For the main attraction, Sandy will perform the

greatest, the scariest, the most _____ feat ever attempted
ADJECTIVE

in Bikini Bottom. We won't tell you what it is—you'll have to see

it with your own two _____—but we guarantee your
PLURAL NOUN

_____will be in your _____ throughout the
PART OF THE BODY   PART OF THE BODY

whole _____ performance. Come one, come all!
ADJECTIVE

MAD LIBS® is fun to play with friends, but you can also play it by yourself! To begin with, DO NOT look at the story on the page below. Fill in the blanks on this page with the words called for. Then, using the words you have selected, fill in the blank spaces in the story.

Now you've created your own hilarious MAD LIBS® game!

THE CASE OF THE MISSING ...

NOUN _____

ADJECTIVE _____

ADVERB _____

NOUN _____

NOUN _____

PLURAL NOUN _____

SAME PLURAL NOUN _____

SAME PLURAL NOUN _____

ADJECTIVE _____

PLURAL NOUN _____

NOUN _____

PLURAL NOUN _____

ADJECTIVE _____

MAD LIBS
THE CASE OF THE MISSING . . .

Lawyer: "Where were you the other night, Plankton?"

Plankton: "I was at home, washing my _____."
                                          NOUN

Lawyer: "A/An _____ story. _____ for you, though, I
                    ADJECTIVE   ADVERB

happen to know that you don't even own a washing _____!
                                                    NOUN

What dastardly _____ are you trying to hide?"
                  NOUN

Plankton: "Nothing! I wasn't anywhere near the Krusty Krab the night

the _____ were stolen!"
      PLURAL NOUN

Lawyer: "How did you know we were here to talk about stolen

_____? I never said anything about stolen _____."
SAME PLURAL NOUN   SAME PLURAL NOUN

Plankton: "Your clever wordplay has trumped my _____
                                                      ADJECTIVE

little mind, and I can't keep my story straight anymore. I confess! I

stole them! Slap the handcuffs on my _____, take me to
                                        PLURAL NOUN

the Big _____, and put me behind _____!
          NOUN   PLURAL NOUN

But you just wait, for I shall be more _____ next time. Oh
                                          ADJECTIVE

yes, there will be a next time!"

MAD LIBS® is fun to play with friends, but you can also play it by yourself! To begin with, DO NOT look at the story on the page below. Fill in the blanks on this page with the words called for. Then, using the words you have selected, fill in the blank spaces in the story.

Now you've created your own hilarious MAD LIBS® game!

SANDY'S SCRAPBOOK

NOUN _____

PLURAL NOUN _____

NOUN _____

ADJECTIVE _____

SILLY WORD _____

PLURAL NOUN _____

NOUN _____

PLURAL NOUN _____

ADVERB _____

PLURAL NOUN _____

NOUN _____

ADJECTIVE _____

PLURAL NOUN _____

NOUN _____

MAD LIBS
SANDY'S SCRAPBOOK

When I was a wee squirrel, I dreamed of being a world-renowned

_____ and exploring new _____. I climbed
    NOUN   PLURAL NOUN

a small _____ and declared that someday, when I was
                NOUN

_____ enough, I would climb Mt. _____—
  ADJECTIVE   SILLY WORD

higher than any squirrel has climbed before. And I did! I also used

to build _____ out of sand on the beach, dreaming that
          PLURAL NOUN

someday I would build a real _____ for underwater
                              NOUN

_____ to enjoy. And I did! Now I live in Bikini Bottom, and
  PLURAL NOUN

I'm still _____ going where no squirrel has gone before.
         ADVERB

I know in my heart of _____ that someday I'll travel to
                     PLURAL NOUN

distant planets in another solar _____, in another galaxy, in
                                  NOUN

a/an _____ universe filled with _____! You
         ADJECTIVE   PLURAL NOUN

can bet your bottom _____ on it!
                     NOUN

From SPONGEBOB SQUAREPANTS™ MAD LIBS® • © 2006 Viacom International Inc.
All Rights Reserved. Nickelodeon, SpongeBob SquarePants and all related titles, logos and characters
are trademarks of Viacom International Inc. Published by Price Stern Sloan, a division of
Penguin Young Readers Group, 345 Hudson Street, New York, New York 10014.

MAD LIBS® is fun to play with friends, but you can also play it by yourself! To begin with, DO NOT look at the story on the page below. Fill in the blanks on this page with the words called for. Then, using the words you have selected, fill in the blank spaces in the story.

Now you've created your own hilarious MAD LIBS® game!

A TOUR OF BIKINI BOTTOM WITH SPONGEBOB

ADJECTIVE _____

VERB _____

PLURAL NOUN _____

ADVERB _____

VERB ENDING IN "ING" _____

PLURAL NOUN _____

ADJECTIVE _____

NOUN _____

PLURAL NOUN _____

VERB ENDING IN "ING" _____

ADJECTIVE _____

OCCUPATION _____

VERB _____

PLURAL NOUN _____

ADJECTIVE _____

MAD LIBS
A TOUR OF BIKINI BOTTOM
WITH SPONGEBOB

If you travel way down deep to the bottom of the sea, you'll find a/an

_____ world where the jellyfish _____ free and the
ADJECTIVE   VERB

_____ grow _____. You've made it to Bikini Bottom!
PLURAL NOUN   ADVERB

I love living here. How much? More than _____ at
              VERB ENDING IN "ING"

Jellyfish Fields. More than eating Krabby _____. More
             PLURAL NOUN

than ... more than Mr. Krabs loves money! I live in a/an _____
               ADJECTIVE

pineapple, and my neighbor Patrick lives under a/an _____.
              NOUN

My two favorite restaurants in Bikini Bottom are the Krusty Krab

and Goofy Goober's, where I eat delicious _____.
            PLURAL NOUN

If you're new to town and hungry, let me be the first to warn you

against _____ at the Chum Bucket—the only item
  VERB ENDING IN "ING"

on the menu is Chumbalaya, and the service is _____. Bikini
             ADJECTIVE

Bottom also has a beach that's guarded by a strong _____.
            OCCUPATION

Everyone goes there to _____ on the waves and build
        VERB

_____. Ah, Bikini Bottom—it's my home, _____
PLURAL NOUN   ADJECTIVE

home!

MAD LIBS® is fun to play with friends, but you can also play it by yourself! To begin with, DO NOT look at the story on the page below. Fill in the blanks on this page with the words called for. Then, using the words you have selected, fill in the blank spaces in the story.

Now you've created your own hilarious MAD LIBS® game!

SANDY'S KARATE LESSON

COLOR _____

SILLY WORD _____

ADVERB _____

NOUN _____

ADJECTIVE _____

NOUN _____

PART OF THE BODY (PLURAL) _____

EXCLAMATION _____

NOUN _____

NOUN _____

ADJECTIVE _____

ADJECTIVE _____

NOUN _____

MAD LIBS®
SANDY'S KARATE LESSON

If you want to be a/an _____ belt in karate (pronounced
COLOR

"kah-rah-tay"), then you must learn the _____ technique,
SILLY WORD

which involves _____ creeping up behind your
ADVERB

opponent's _____. You wait until he or she least expects it,
NOUN

and then *bam*! You break out all your _____ karate moves.
ADJECTIVE

There's nothing to it really, except you must remember to be as quiet as

a/an _____ and walk on your tippy-_____
NOUN   PART OF THE BODY (PLURAL)

so you don't ruin the surprise. Also, remember to shout "Hiiiiiiya!"

which is Japanese for "_____!" This shows your
EXCLAMATION

_____ that you mean business. Watch me demonstrate
NOUN

this technique on SpongeBob. He's helping Squidward paint his

_____ today and won't suspect a thing! (Sandy performs the
NOUN

move. We hear "Hiiiiiiya!" and "Eek!" followed by a/an _____
                                                        ADJECTIVE

crash.) Sorry! That reminds me, folks, always practice in a/an

_____ area, far away from Squidward's favorite
ADJECTIVE

_____ ... Oops!
NOUN

MAD LIBS® is fun to play with friends, but you can also play it by yourself! To begin with, DO NOT look at the story on the page below. Fill in the blanks on this page with the words called for. Then, using the words you have selected, fill in the blank spaces in the story.

Now you've created your own hilarious MAD LIBS® game!

KRABBY PATTY SECRET FORMULA

ADJECTIVE _____

VERB ENDING IN "ING" _____

ADJECTIVE _____

NOUN _____

NOUN _____

PLURAL NOUN _____

PLURAL NOUN _____

ADVERB _____

PLURAL NOUN _____

VERB _____

NUMBER _____

TYPE OF LIQUID _____

ADJECTIVE _____

NOUN _____

NUMBER _____

PLURAL NOUN _____

PLURAL NOUN _____

ADJECTIVE _____

MAD LIBS

KRABBY PATTY SECRET FORMULA

Have you ever wondered what's really in the Krusty Krab's

_____ Krabby Patties? After much _____
   ADJECTIVE   VERB ENDING IN "ING"

with different recipes in the kitchen, we've discovered the

_____ formula! First you mix 1 teaspoon of crushed
  ADJECTIVE

_____ with 2 cups of boiled _____
    NOUN   NOUN

broth. Then take 5 _____ and 2 _____ and add
               PLURAL NOUN   PLURAL NOUN

them in. Stir _____. Shape the mixture into individual
              ADVERB

_____ and place them in the oven. Let the mixture
  PLURAL NOUN

_____ at _____ degrees. Meanwhile, prepare
   VERB   NUMBER

the buns by mixing 2 tablespoons of _____ with
                               TYPE OF LIQUID

5 cups of _____ flour. Knead the dough into a/an
           ADJECTIVE

_____ and then bake. In just _____ minutes,
  NOUN   NUMBER

they should be ready. Let the _____ cool. Put the patties on
                         PLURAL NOUN

the buns, add ketchup and _____ on top, and you've got
                    PLURAL NOUN

yourself a/an _____ Krabby Patty! *Bon appétit!*
         ADJECTIVE